Table Of Contents

Chapter 2: Sustainable Investing 1
Chapter 3: Cryptocurrency Investing 1
Chapter 4: Real Estate Investing 1
Chapter 5: Dividend Growth Investing 1
Chapter 6: Small-Cap Stock Investing 1
Chapter 7: International Market Investing... 1
Chapter 8: Building a Global Investment Portfolio 1
Chapter 9: Resources and Tools for Investors 1
Chapter 10: Conclusion: Embracing Global Opportunities 1
Chapter 1: Introduction to Global Opportunities 1

Chapter 1: Introduction to Global Opportunities

Understanding Global Markets

Understanding global markets is essential for anyone looking to navigate the complexities of international investing. The interconnectedness of economies around the world means that events in one region can have far-reaching implications elsewhere. For parents, teachers, and students, grasping the dynamics of global markets can empower them to make informed investment decisions. This understanding is particularly relevant in today's fast-paced world, where sustainable investing, cryptocurrency, and real estate are gaining traction.

Sustainable investing focuses on generating financial returns while promoting social and environmental good. As global awareness of climate change and social responsibility increases, companies that prioritize sustainability often present strong investment opportunities. Understanding the global market allows investors to identify regions and sectors that prioritize green initiatives. This is valuable for new parents who want to align their financial choices with their values, ensuring a healthier planet for future generations.

Cryptocurrency investing has emerged as a revolutionary approach to finance, attracting attention from diverse demographics. The global nature of cryptocurrencies means that they are not limited by traditional borders, making them accessible to anyone with an internet connection. Understanding how global markets influence cryptocurrency trends can enhance investment strategies. For college students and young professionals looking to build wealth, grasping the volatility and opportunities within the crypto space is crucial for navigating this innovative investment frontier.

Real estate investing is another area where global market insights can prove beneficial. Real estate trends often reflect broader economic indicators, such as interest rates, employment rates, and population growth. By understanding these global factors, investors can make more strategic decisions about where to buy properties. For new moms and dads, investing in real estate can create a stable financial foundation for their family, and recognizing how international markets impact local real estate values can yield significant advantages.

Dividend growth investing and small-cap stock investing are also influenced by global market conditions. Companies that consistently increase dividends often demonstrate resilience and stable growth, providing a reliable income stream for investors. Meanwhile, small-cap stocks can be more volatile, but they also offer the potential for substantial gains as they expand. Parents and teachers can benefit from understanding how these investment strategies are affected by global economic trends, enabling them to mentor students or make informed decisions for their families' financial futures. Recognizing the interplay between global markets and these investment niches can lead to more strategic, informed choices in the pursuit of financial goals.

The Importance of Diversification

Diversification is a fundamental principle in investing that significantly reduces risk while maximizing potential returns. For parents, teachers, college students, and new moms and dads, understanding the importance of diversification is crucial, especially as they navigate their financial futures. In an ever-evolving global market, putting all your financial resources into one type of investment can lead to substantial losses. By spreading investments across different asset classes, such as sustainable investing, cryptocurrency, real estate, dividend growth, small-cap stocks, and international markets, investors can create a balanced portfolio that withstands market fluctuations.

One of the key benefits of diversification is its ability to mitigate risks. Markets can be unpredictable, and sectors can experience downturns due to various factors like economic changes, regulations, or natural disasters. By diversifying across various investment avenues, individuals can shield themselves from the adverse impacts of a single market decline. For instance, while the cryptocurrency market may be experiencing volatility, investments in dividend growth or real estate can provide stability and consistent income, helping to maintain overall portfolio health.

Moreover, diversification allows investors to tap into different growth opportunities that various markets offer. Sustainable investing is gaining traction as more people prioritize ethical considerations in their financial decisions. By including sustainable investments in a diversified portfolio, investors not only contribute positively to society but also position themselves to benefit from a growing sector. Similarly, small-cap stocks often provide unique growth potential that larger, established companies may not offer. A well-diversified portfolio can leverage these opportunities, maximizing returns over time.

Investing in international markets is another critical aspect of diversification. Different countries and regions may perform well during various economic cycles, and by including international investments, investors can take advantage of global growth trends. This geographic diversification adds an additional layer of protection, as economic downturns in one country may not necessarily impact assets in another. Parents and new moms and dads, in particular, can benefit from this strategy, as it may provide more stability for their family's financial future.

In conclusion, the importance of diversification cannot be overstated, especially in today's complex financial landscape. By understanding and implementing a diversified investment strategy, individuals can protect their assets while positioning themselves for long-term growth. Whether through sustainable investing, cryptocurrency, real estate, or other avenues, a diversified portfolio empowers parents, teachers, college students, and new families to navigate the international market with confidence, ensuring they can achieve their financial goals while securing a brighter future for themselves and their loved ones.

Key Trends Shaping International Investing

As the world becomes increasingly interconnected, international investing has gained significant traction among various demographics, including parents, teachers, and young families. One of the most prominent trends is the rise of sustainable investing. This approach prioritizes investments that not only yield financial returns but also positively impact the environment and society. With millennials and Generation Z leading the charge, there is a growing demand for companies that adhere to Environmental, Social, and

Governance (ESG) criteria. This trend encourages investors to consider the broader implications of their financial choices, fostering a generation that is both socially conscious and financially savvy.

Another key trend reshaping the landscape of international investing is the surge of cryptocurrency. As digital currencies like Bitcoin and Ethereum gain legitimacy, they present unique opportunities for diversification in an investment portfolio. For many new parents and college students, cryptocurrency represents an accessible entry point into the world of investing, often requiring lower capital outlays compared to traditional asset classes. The volatility of cryptocurrencies can be daunting, but their potential for high returns is appealing. Understanding blockchain technology and the regulatory environment surrounding digital currencies is essential for anyone looking to capitalize on this trend.

Real estate investing continues to be a favored avenue for international investors, particularly in emerging markets. As urbanization accelerates globally, opportunities in real estate—whether through direct ownership, Real Estate Investment Trusts (REITs), or crowdfunding platforms—are becoming more attractive. Young families may find that investing in international properties can provide both rental income and long-term appreciation. Moreover, global real estate markets often react differently to economic conditions, allowing investors to hedge against downturns in their home markets. The key is to conduct thorough research and assess local regulations and market trends before committing capital.

Dividend growth investing is another trend that appeals to a wide audience, especially those seeking passive income. This strategy focuses on companies with a history of increasing their dividends, providing a reliable income stream while potentially capitalizing on capital appreciation. Parents and teachers, looking for stability in their investment portfolios, may find this approach particularly appealing as it combines both growth and income. Furthermore, international markets often present unique dividend opportunities, allowing investors to diversify their income sources and reduce reliance on domestic dividends.

Finally, small-cap stock investing is gaining attention as investors seek high-growth potential in international markets. Small-cap companies, often overlooked by large institutional investors, can offer substantial rewards as they expand and innovate. For college students and new moms and dads, investing in small-cap stocks can be an exciting way to engage with the market and support emerging businesses. While this strategy carries higher risks, the possibility of significant returns makes it an attractive option for those willing to do their homework. By staying informed about market trends and the global economic landscape, investors can position themselves to take advantage of the dynamic opportunities presented by small-cap stocks.

Chapter 2: Sustainable Investing

Defining Sustainable Investing

Sustainable investing refers to investment strategies that consider environmental, social, and governance (ESG) factors alongside financial returns. This approach aims to generate long-term financial gains while promoting positive societal impact and sustainable practices. For parents, teachers, and college students, understanding sustainable investing offers an opportunity to align personal values with investment choices. By focusing on companies that prioritize sustainability, individuals can contribute to a healthier planet and society while potentially benefiting from the growth of these forward-thinking businesses.

At the heart of sustainable investing is the belief that companies actively engaged in responsible practices can outperform their peers over time. This stems from the recognition that sustainability risks, such as climate change and social inequality, can significantly impact financial performance. For new moms and dads looking to secure their family's financial future, sustainable investing provides a pathway to invest in industries that are poised for growth as the demand for eco-friendly products and services increases. By choosing sustainable investments, families can support companies that are making a difference while working towards their financial goals.

There are various strategies within sustainable investing, including negative screening, positive screening, and impact investing. Negative screening involves excluding companies that do not meet certain ethical criteria, such as those involved in fossil fuels or tobacco. Positive screening, on the other hand, focuses on selecting companies that actively promote sustainability through innovative practices, such as renewable energy or waste reduction. Impact investing takes this further by targeting investments that generate measurable social or environmental benefits alongside financial returns. Educators and college students can explore these strategies to better understand how their investment choices can reflect their values.

One significant aspect of sustainable investing is the increasing availability of data and tools that help investors assess ESG factors. Platforms now offer insights into a company's sustainability practices, allowing investors to make informed decisions. This development is particularly beneficial for parents who want to teach their children about responsible finance. By integrating lessons on sustainable investing into educational curricula, teachers can equip students with the knowledge to navigate an evolving financial landscape, emphasizing the importance of ethical decision-making in investments.

As the global economy shifts towards more sustainable practices, the opportunities for sustainable investing are expected to grow. Industries such as renewable energy, sustainable agriculture, and green technology are gaining traction, promising not only environmental benefits but also substantial financial returns. For families considering their investment strategies, embracing sustainable investing can lead to a more secure financial future while contributing to a better world. Understanding these concepts will empower individuals across various demographics to become informed investors who prioritize both profit and purpose.

Benefits of Sustainable Investments

Sustainable investments have emerged as a dynamic and critical avenue for individuals seeking to align their financial goals with their values. One of the primary benefits of sustainable investing is the potential for long-term financial returns. Research has consistently shown that companies committed to environmental, social, and governance (ESG) principles often outperform their peers in traditional sectors. This trend is driven by a growing consumer preference for responsible brands, which can lead to increased sales and brand loyalty. For parents, teachers, and new moms and dads, investing in companies that prioritize sustainability not only supports a healthier planet but can also provide a promising financial future for their families.

Another significant benefit of sustainable investing is the reduced risk associated with companies that adhere to ESG criteria. Firms that actively manage their environmental impact, social responsibilities, and governance practices are often better equipped to navigate regulatory changes and market shifts. This resilience can protect investors from potential losses linked to companies that fail to adapt to evolving standards and expectations. For college students and young professionals, understanding the importance of such risk management can guide them toward making informed investment choices that safeguard their financial well-being while supporting ethical business practices.

Sustainable investments also foster innovation and drive the growth of new industries, particularly in renewable energy and technology. As the world moves toward a more sustainable future, companies that invest in clean technologies and sustainable practices are likely to see substantial growth opportunities. This creates a fertile ground for small-cap stock investing, allowing investors to capitalize on emerging companies that are leading the charge in sustainability. For those looking to diversify their portfolios, including sustainable investments can enhance overall returns while contributing to positive societal change.

Moreover, sustainable investing encourages greater corporate transparency and accountability. As investors increasingly demand higher standards of ESG performance, companies are motivated to disclose more information about their practices and impacts. This shift not only benefits investors by providing clearer insights into potential risks and opportunities but also empowers consumers and communities. Parents and educators can leverage this information to teach younger generations about the importance of corporate responsibility and the role they can play as informed consumers and investors in shaping a better world.

Finally, sustainable investing aligns with the values of many individuals who seek to make a positive impact through their financial choices. By investing in companies that prioritize sustainability, investors can contribute to environmental preservation, social equity, and ethical governance. This alignment of values can enhance personal fulfillment and satisfaction, knowing that their investments support a future that reflects their beliefs. As parents, teachers, and new moms and dads look to the future, sustainable investing offers a pathway not only to financial growth but also to fostering a legacy of responsibility and care for the planet and society.

How to Identify Sustainable Companies

Identifying sustainable companies is crucial for investors seeking to align their portfolios with their values, particularly as global awareness of environmental and social issues grows. To begin, one can examine a company's commitment to sustainability through its environmental, social, and governance (ESG) criteria. These criteria provide a framework for evaluating a company's ethical impact and sustainability practices. Investors should look for businesses that actively measure and disclose their carbon emissions, energy usage, and resource conservation efforts. Firms that engage in transparent reporting are often more trustworthy and show a genuine commitment to sustainability.

Another important factor in identifying sustainable companies is their involvement in renewable energy and resource efficiency initiatives. Companies that invest in clean technologies or employ sustainable practices in their operations tend to be more resilient in the face of regulatory changes and shifting consumer preferences. For instance, firms that have adopted circular economy principles, which focus on reducing waste and reusing materials, often demonstrate forward-thinking strategies that can yield long-term benefits. Recognizing businesses that prioritize innovation in sustainability can provide investors with opportunities in industries poised for growth.

Social responsibility is equally vital in assessing a company's sustainability. This includes evaluating how a company treats its employees, suppliers, and the communities in which it operates. Companies committed to fair labor practices, diversity and inclusion, and community engagement are typically more sustainable in the long run. Investors should seek out firms that have strong policies regarding employee rights and community development, as these traits often correlate with a positive corporate reputation and lower risk of scandals or negative publicity.

Governance structures also play a significant role in identifying sustainable companies. A strong governance framework ensures that a company is managed effectively and ethically, which is essential for long-term sustainability. Investors should analyze the composition of a company's board of directors, looking for diversity and expertise in sustainability-related fields. Additionally, companies with robust policies against corruption and a commitment to ethical business practices are more likely to maintain their sustainability objectives and achieve financial success.

Lastly, leveraging third-party ratings and indices can aid in identifying sustainable companies. Various organizations evaluate and rank companies based on their sustainability practices, providing investors with valuable insights. Resources such as the Dow Jones Sustainability Index or MSCI ESG Ratings can serve as starting points for discovering businesses that meet sustainability criteria. By utilizing these tools alongside personal research, investors can make informed decisions that support sustainable growth and contribute to a more responsible global economy.

Case Studies in Sustainable Investing

Sustainable investing has gained considerable traction over the past decade, driven by a growing awareness of environmental, social, and governance (ESG) factors. Case studies in this field illustrate how investors can align their portfolios with their values while still achieving financial returns. One notable example is the rise of green bonds, which are specifically earmarked for projects that have positive environmental impacts. The World Bank issued its first green bond in 2008, and since then, the market has expanded significantly, attracting both institutional and retail investors looking to support renewable energy initiatives and sustainable infrastructure.

Another compelling case study is the performance of socially responsible mutual funds compared to their traditional counterparts. Research indicates that funds focusing on companies with strong ESG practices often outperform the market average. For instance, a study conducted by Morningstar found that sustainable funds outperformed traditional funds during market downturns, demonstrating resilience during challenging economic conditions. This trend suggests that integrating sustainability into investment strategies does not merely serve ethical considerations but can also enhance risk-adjusted returns.

The impact of sustainable investing extends beyond financial performance; it also influences corporate behavior. Companies that adopt sustainable practices tend to foster innovation and improve their operational efficiencies. A case in point is Unilever, which has committed to a sustainable living plan aimed at reducing its environmental footprint while enhancing social impact. By prioritizing sustainability, Unilever has not only attracted socially conscious investors but also improved its brand reputation and customer loyalty, ultimately leading to increased profitability.

Real estate investing provides another lens through which to examine sustainable practices. Projects that focus on energy efficiency and sustainable building materials are becoming increasingly popular. For instance, the Bullitt Center in Seattle is often referred to as the greenest commercial building in the world. It utilizes solar panels for energy, rainwater harvesting systems, and composting toilets. Investors in such sustainable real estate projects are not only contributing to environmental preservation but also tapping into a growing market demand for green buildings, which often command higher rents and occupancy rates.

Lastly, the advent of technology in sustainable investing is exemplified by the rise of impact investing platforms that allow individual investors to contribute to projects with measurable social or environmental outcomes. Platforms such as StartSomeGood and Kiva enable users to finance startups and entrepreneurs focused on sustainability. These case studies highlight the diverse opportunities available in sustainable investing, demonstrating that it is possible to achieve financial returns while making a positive impact on the world. As awareness of sustainability continues to grow, the integration of these principles into investment strategies is likely to become the norm rather than the exception.

Chapter 3: Cryptocurrency Investing

What is Cryptocurrency?

Cryptocurrency is a form of digital or virtual currency that uses cryptography for security, making it difficult to counterfeit or double-spend. It operates on a technology called blockchain, which is a decentralized ledger that records all transactions across a network of computers. This technology ensures transparency and security, as each transaction is linked to previous ones, creating a chain that is virtually immutable. Unlike traditional currencies issued by governments, cryptocurrencies are not controlled by any central authority, which gives them unique features and appeals to various investors.

The most well-known cryptocurrency is Bitcoin, created in 2009 by an anonymous individual or group of individuals using the pseudonym Satoshi Nakamoto. Bitcoin was designed as an alternative to traditional currencies and aimed to provide a peer-to-peer payment system that would operate independently of central banks. Since then, thousands of other cryptocurrencies have emerged, each with their own unique features and purposes.

Some, like Ethereum, enable the creation of smart contracts and decentralized applications, while others focus on enhancing privacy or facilitating specific industries.

Investing in cryptocurrencies has gained popularity among various demographics, including parents and college students, due to the potential for high returns and the growing acceptance of digital currencies in the mainstream financial ecosystem. However, it is important for new investors to approach cryptocurrency with caution. The market is known for its volatility, with prices often experiencing rapid fluctuations. Understanding the risks and benefits associated with cryptocurrency investing is crucial for making informed decisions, especially for those who may be new to the world of finance.

For parents and educators, introducing the concept of cryptocurrency can be an opportunity to discuss broader themes of financial literacy and technology. As digital currencies become more integrated into everyday transactions, understanding how they function and their implications for the economy becomes increasingly important. Conversations about cryptocurrency can also lead to discussions about responsible investing, the importance of research, and the need to develop a diversified investment strategy that includes various asset classes.

As sustainable investing gains traction, the intersection of cryptocurrency and environmental concerns is also worth exploring. Some cryptocurrencies, like Bitcoin, have faced criticism for their energy-intensive mining processes. However, other projects are emerging that prioritize sustainability, using alternative consensus mechanisms that require significantly less energy. For parents and educators, examining these developments can foster critical thinking about the future of finance and technology, encouraging the next generation to consider not only the potential returns of their investments but also their social and environmental impact.

The Rise of Digital Currency

The rise of digital currency marks a significant shift in the global financial landscape, captivating the attention of investors and consumers alike. As traditional banking systems face challenges in adapting to rapid technological advancements, digital currencies have emerged as a viable alternative. These currencies, such as Bitcoin and Ethereum, offer decentralized financial transactions that bypass traditional financial institutions. This shift not only democratizes finance but also opens up new avenues for investment, especially for those interested in sustainable, cryptocurrency, and international market investing.

One of the key factors driving the popularity of digital currencies is their potential for high returns. Early investors in cryptocurrencies have seen extraordinary gains, prompting many to consider them as alternative investments. Digital currencies are particularly appealing to younger generations, including college students and new parents, who are often more tech-savvy and willing to embrace innovative financial solutions. As the market for digital currencies continues to mature, educational resources and investment platforms are becoming more accessible, empowering individuals from various backgrounds to participate in this evolving landscape.

Moreover, the integration of blockchain technology, which underpins most digital currencies, enhances security and transparency in transactions. This technology not only mitigates fraud risks but also allows for the tracking of digital assets in a way that traditional currencies cannot match. For parents and educators, understanding blockchain and its implications for future financial systems can provide valuable insights into preparing the next generation for a rapidly changing economic environment. As digital currencies gain traction, it is essential for individuals to be informed about the underlying technologies that support them.

Sustainable investing is another area where digital currencies are making a mark. Many new cryptocurrencies are designed with environmentally friendly practices in mind, seeking to reduce energy consumption and carbon footprints associated with mining operations. This focus on sustainability aligns with the values of many investors today, particularly new moms and dads who are concerned about the future of the planet for their children. By exploring digital currencies that emphasize sustainability, investors can align their financial goals with their ethical beliefs, contributing to a more responsible investment landscape.

Finally, the global nature of digital currencies offers unique opportunities for international market investing. Unlike traditional assets, which may be influenced by local economic conditions, digital currencies provide access to a borderless financial ecosystem. This characteristic enables investors to diversify their portfolios beyond national markets and participate in global trends. For parents and educators, fostering an understanding of international investment strategies, particularly in the context of digital currencies, can equip future generations with the knowledge needed to navigate and thrive in an interconnected world. As the rise of digital currency continues, it is crucial for individuals to stay informed and engaged with these transformative developments.

Risks and Rewards of Cryptocurrency

Cryptocurrency has emerged as a significant player in the global financial landscape, presenting both enticing opportunities and notable risks. For parents, teachers, and college students exploring investment options, understanding these dynamics is crucial. The decentralized nature of cryptocurrencies, such as Bitcoin and Ethereum, offers a new form of digital currency that can be traded and utilized across borders. This innovation enables investors to participate in a rapidly evolving market that can provide substantial returns. However, the volatility and unpredictability of cryptocurrency prices can lead to significant financial losses, making it essential for potential investors to weigh these factors carefully.

One of the primary rewards of investing in cryptocurrency is the potential for high returns. Cryptocurrencies have shown remarkable growth rates, with early adopters often reaping significant profits. For example, Bitcoin, which started as a niche digital currency, has reached substantial valuations over the years. This growth potential attracts many new investors, including young parents looking to secure their children's financial futures or college students wanting to build wealth early. Furthermore, the rise of decentralized finance (DeFi) platforms and non-fungible tokens (NFTs) has expanded the scope of investment opportunities within the cryptocurrency sphere, appealing to those interested in sustainable and innovative investment strategies.

Conversely, the risks associated with cryptocurrency investing cannot be overlooked. The market is known for its extreme volatility, with prices experiencing wild fluctuations within short periods. This unpredictability can lead to emotional decision-making, which may result in poor investment choices. Additionally, the lack of regulation in the cryptocurrency market raises concerns about security and fraud. Investors, particularly those who are new to the space, may fall victim to scams or lose their assets due to hacking incidents. Parents and educators must emphasize the importance of thorough research and risk management when approaching this investment avenue.

Another critical factor is the regulatory landscape surrounding cryptocurrencies. Governments worldwide are still developing frameworks to govern cryptocurrency trading and usage, which can create uncertainty for investors. Regulatory changes can significantly impact the value of cryptocurrencies, as seen in instances where countries have imposed strict regulations or outright bans. This evolving environment can be daunting for new investors, especially for parents concerned about the long-term viability of their investments. Staying informed about regulatory developments is essential for anyone considering entering the cryptocurrency market.

In conclusion, the risks and rewards of cryptocurrency investing present a complex picture for potential investors. While the allure of high returns and innovative financial products can be enticing, the volatility and regulatory uncertainties pose significant challenges. For parents, teachers, and college students, a balanced approach that includes education, research, and risk management is vital. By understanding both the opportunities and pitfalls associated with cryptocurrency, investors can make informed decisions that align with their financial goals and values, paving the way for a more secure financial future in an increasingly digital world.

Strategies for Investing in Cryptocurrencies

Investing in cryptocurrencies requires a thoughtful approach, especially for parents, teachers, and college students who are navigating their financial futures. To begin, it is crucial to educate oneself about the basics of blockchain technology and the various types of cryptocurrencies available in the market. Understanding the underlying technology can help demystify the complexities of cryptocurrencies and enable investors to make informed decisions. There are numerous online resources, courses, and community forums dedicated to cryptocurrency education that can serve as a foundation for new investors.

Once familiar with the landscape, it's important to develop a clear investment strategy. This involves defining personal financial goals, risk tolerance, and investment timelines. For example, parents planning for their children's education may prefer a more conservative approach, focusing on established cryptocurrencies like Bitcoin or Ethereum. In contrast, younger investors or college students looking for higher potential returns might consider allocating a portion of their portfolio to smaller, emerging cryptocurrencies. Diversification is key; spreading investments across various cryptocurrencies can mitigate risk and enhance potential rewards.

Analyzing market trends and staying updated on the latest developments in the cryptocurrency space is essential for making informed investment decisions. Investors should follow reputable news sources, join cryptocurrency communities, and participate in discussions on social media platforms. Understanding market sentiment, regulatory changes, and technological advancements can provide valuable insights that influence the performance of specific cryptocurrencies. Additionally, keeping an eye on major events, such as forks or major partnerships, can help investors capitalize on potential opportunities.

Implementing risk management strategies is another vital component of successful cryptocurrency investing. Setting stop-loss orders, which automatically sell a cryptocurrency when it reaches a certain price, can protect investments from significant losses. Investors should also consider not investing more than they can afford to lose, especially in such a volatile market. Regularly reviewing and adjusting one's portfolio based on performance and market conditions can help maintain a balanced approach and align with long-term financial goals.

Lastly, engaging with a community of like-minded investors can provide support and shared knowledge, essential for navigating the unpredictable cryptocurrency market. Online forums, local meetups, and investment clubs can facilitate discussions and offer valuable insights. For parents and educators, fostering an environment where students can learn about cryptocurrency investing together can stimulate interest in financial literacy and sustainable investment practices. By sharing experiences and strategies, individuals can empower one another to make informed choices and achieve their financial aspirations in the exciting world of cryptocurrencies.

Chapter 4: Real Estate Investing

The Basics of Real Estate Investing

Real estate investing is a time-tested method for building wealth and securing financial futures. At its core, it involves purchasing, owning, managing, renting, or selling properties for profit. There are various types of real estate investments, including residential, commercial, industrial, and raw land. Each category offers unique opportunities and challenges, allowing investors to choose a path that aligns with their financial goals and risk tolerance. Understanding the fundamentals of real estate can empower individuals, including parents, teachers, and students, to make informed decisions in their investment journeys.

One of the key concepts in real estate investing is the principle of location. The adage "location, location, location" underscores the importance of geographic factors in property value. Properties in desirable neighborhoods or those close to amenities like schools, parks, and shopping centers tend to appreciate more rapidly and attract higher rental yields. For new moms and dads or families looking to invest, understanding local market trends and demographics can help identify areas with growth potential, ensuring a sound investment.

Financing is another crucial aspect of real estate investing. Most investors leverage mortgages to purchase properties, which allows them to control larger assets while minimizing upfront cash requirements. Different financing options, such as conventional loans, FHA loans, or even creative financing methods like seller financing, can be explored. It's important for potential investors to understand their financial situation and creditworthiness, as these factors will influence the types of loans available to them and the terms of those loans.

Investors should also consider the ongoing costs associated with real estate ownership. These can include property taxes, insurance, maintenance, and management fees. For those investing in rental properties, calculating potential rental income against these costs is essential for determining profitability. Additionally, understanding the legal aspects of real estate, such as tenant rights and landlord obligations, is critical to managing properties effectively and avoiding legal issues that can arise from mismanagement.

Finally, the role of market research cannot be overstated in real estate investing. Regularly monitoring trends in property values, rental rates, and economic indicators can provide insights into when to buy or sell properties. For college students and young professionals interested in sustainable investing, exploring eco-friendly properties or those in green developments can align personal values with financial goals. By gaining a solid understanding of these basics, anyone can embark on a rewarding journey in real estate investing, tapping into its potential for long-term wealth creation.

International Real Estate Markets

International real estate markets present a unique landscape for investors, characterized by diverse opportunities and challenges.

Understanding the dynamics of these markets is crucial for anyone looking to expand their investment portfolios beyond domestic boundaries. Factors such as economic stability, government regulations, and cultural nuances play significant roles in shaping international real estate. Investors must also consider the potential for growth in emerging markets, where rapid urbanization and increasing demand for housing can yield substantial returns.

One of the key advantages of investing in international real estate is the potential for diversification. By spreading investments across various countries, investors can mitigate risks associated with local market fluctuations. For instance, if one country's economy faces a downturn, properties in another stable or growing economy may continue to appreciate. This diversification can be particularly appealing to families and individuals planning for long-term financial security, as it provides a buffer against domestic economic uncertainties.

Sustainable investing has gained momentum globally, and international real estate markets are no exception. Investors are increasingly looking for properties that meet environmental standards and contribute positively to communities. This trend is not only beneficial for the planet but can also enhance property values as demand for eco-friendly buildings rises. For new parents and families, investing in sustainable real estate can be a way to ensure a healthier future for their children while securing financial returns.

Cryptocurrency has emerged as a novel investment tool, and its integration into international real estate transactions is gaining traction. Blockchain technology offers transparency and efficiency in property dealings, making it easier for investors to conduct cross-border transactions. New moms and dads, who are often tech-savvy and interested in innovative investment strategies, may find this intersection of cryptocurrency and real estate appealing. Understanding how to leverage these technologies can open new avenues for investment and facilitate entry into international markets.

Finally, it is essential for potential investors to conduct thorough research and due diligence when exploring international real estate. Each market has its own legal frameworks, taxation policies, and cultural considerations that can impact investment outcomes. Engaging with local experts, real estate professionals, or investment advisors familiar with international markets can provide invaluable insights. By approaching international real estate with a well-informed strategy, investors can capitalize on global opportunities while navigating the complexities of this multifaceted landscape.

Financing Real Estate Investments

Financing real estate investments is a critical aspect for anyone looking to delve into this lucrative market, particularly for those who may be new to investing. Understanding the various financing options available can empower parents, teachers, college students, and new moms and dads to make informed decisions that align with their financial goals. Traditional financing methods, such as mortgages from banks or credit unions, remain popular. These loans typically require a down payment, a good credit score, and proof of income. However, as the real estate market evolves, alternative financing options are emerging, offering flexibility and accessibility to a broader audience.

One alternative gaining traction is seller financing, where the property owner acts as the lender. This arrangement can be particularly beneficial for buyers who may struggle to secure traditional financing due to credit issues or lack of sufficient capital. In seller financing, terms are negotiable, allowing buyers to set up payment plans that suit their financial situations. This method can also appeal to sellers looking to expedite the sale process, as it can reduce the time spent on traditional financing hurdles.

Another innovative financing approach is crowdfunding. Real estate crowdfunding platforms allow multiple investors to pool their resources to fund a property purchase or project. This method opens up opportunities for those with limited capital to invest in real estate without needing substantial upfront funds. Crowdfunding not only diversifies investment portfolios but also provides exposure to various real estate markets and types of properties, making it an attractive option for families and individuals interested in sustainable investing or international markets.

For those interested in integrating modern technology into their investment strategies, cryptocurrency has started to play a role in real estate financing. Certain platforms now accept cryptocurrencies as a form of payment for property transactions, appealing to tech-savvy investors. This method can facilitate quicker transactions and lower fees, thereby reducing the barriers to entry for first-time buyers. As cryptocurrencies continue to gain acceptance, they offer a unique avenue for financing real estate investments, particularly in markets where traditional banking systems may be less accessible.

Ultimately, understanding the diverse financing options available is essential for anyone venturing into real estate investments. Whether considering traditional mortgages, exploring seller financing, engaging in crowdfunding, or utilizing cryptocurrencies, investors must evaluate their unique financial situations and long-term goals. By doing so, parents, teachers, college students, and new moms and dads can unlock the potential of real estate investing while contributing to a more sustainable and diversified investment portfolio.

Trends in Global Real Estate

The global real estate market has seen significant shifts in recent years, influenced by various factors including technological advancements, demographic changes, and evolving consumer preferences. One prominent trend is the increasing demand for sustainable properties. Environmental consciousness has become a priority for many buyers and investors, leading to a surge in green building practices and energy-efficient designs. This trend not only appeals to environmentally-minded individuals but also often results in long-term savings on utility costs, making sustainable real estate an attractive option for families and investors alike.

Another noteworthy trend in global real estate is the integration of technology into property management and investment strategies. Smart home technology, virtual reality tours, and data analytics are transforming how real estate transactions are conducted. For example, virtual reality allows potential buyers to tour properties from anywhere in the world, reducing the need for physical visits and broadening the market reach for sellers. Additionally, property management software streamlines operations and improves tenant experiences, contributing to higher retention rates and overall profitability for investors.

Cryptocurrency is also making waves in the real estate sector, altering traditional investment dynamics. The potential for blockchain technology to facilitate secure, transparent transactions is enticing many investors. This innovation allows for fractional ownership of properties, enabling individuals to invest in real estate without needing substantial capital upfront. For new moms and dads, this could present an opportunity to diversify their investment portfolios with relatively lower financial barriers, aligning with modern investment trends that emphasize accessibility and innovation.

In the context of international market investing, global real estate is becoming increasingly appealing due to favorable exchange rates and economic stability in certain regions. Investors are now looking beyond their domestic markets to capitalize on opportunities in emerging economies where property values are expected to rise. This trend is particularly relevant for young families and college students who may be considering future relocation or investment strategies that include international real estate as part of their financial planning.

Lastly, the rise of remote work has reshaped real estate demand, with many individuals and families seeking properties in suburban or rural areas that offer more space and a better quality of life. This shift has led to increased interest in vacation homes and investment properties outside of urban centers, as people prioritize lifestyle changes and work-life balance. For educators and parents, understanding these trends can guide them in making informed decisions about their own investments or in advising the next generation on navigating the evolving landscape of global real estate.

Chapter 5: Dividend Growth Investing

Introduction to Dividend Growth

Dividend growth investing is a strategy that appeals to a wide range of investors, including parents, teachers, college students, and new moms and dads, as it offers a reliable way to build wealth over time. At its core, this approach focuses on purchasing shares of companies that consistently increase their dividend payouts. For those seeking a stable income stream, particularly in an unpredictable economic environment, dividend growth investing provides an attractive solution. It allows investors to benefit from both capital appreciation and the compounding effect of reinvested dividends, making it a powerful tool for long-term financial planning.

Understanding the mechanics of dividend growth is essential for investors looking to incorporate this strategy into their portfolios. Dividends are payments made by corporations to their shareholders, typically derived from profits. Companies that prioritize dividend growth tend to be financially stable and have a track record of generating consistent earnings. By selecting firms with a history of increasing dividends, investors can create a portfolio that not only yields immediate income but also has the potential for significant growth as companies expand and increase their payouts over time.

For parents and educators, dividend growth investing can serve as an educational tool to teach children and young adults about financial responsibility and the importance of long-term planning. By involving younger generations in the investment process, they can learn valuable lessons about saving, investing, and the power of compound interest from an early age. As families explore sustainable investing options, dividend growth stocks can often be found within companies that prioritize social responsibility, aligning financial goals with ethical considerations.

In the context of global markets, dividend growth investing offers unique opportunities in international markets. Investors can explore companies in emerging economies that may provide higher growth rates and dividend yields compared to their domestic counterparts. This diversification not only enhances potential returns but also spreads risk across various markets and industries. Understanding the global landscape allows investors to make informed decisions and capitalize on trends that may not be available in their local markets.

Finally, as new moms and dads navigate the challenges of family life, establishing a dividend growth investing strategy can be a proactive step toward securing their family's financial future. Whether saving for a child's education, planning for retirement, or simply building wealth, dividend growth investing can provide a sense of security. By focusing on companies with a strong commitment to increasing dividends, parents can set a foundation for their family's financial well-being, ensuring that their investments grow alongside their family's needs and aspirations.

Benefits of Dividend Stocks

Dividend stocks represent a compelling investment opportunity for those seeking a reliable income stream while simultaneously building wealth over time. For parents, teachers, and new moms and dads, understanding the benefits of dividend stocks can provide a pathway to financial stability and growth. Unlike traditional stocks that rely solely on capital appreciation, dividend stocks distribute a portion of their earnings back to shareholders, creating a steady cash flow that can be reinvested or used for everyday expenses. This characteristic makes dividend stocks particularly appealing for individuals looking to balance their financial responsibilities with investment goals.

One of the primary advantages of dividend stocks is their potential for compound growth. By reinvesting dividends, investors can purchase additional shares over time, amplifying their investment returns. This compounding effect can significantly enhance long-term wealth accumulation, especially for college students and young professionals who have the advantage of time on their side. The earlier one begins investing in dividend stocks, the more pronounced the benefits of compounding can be, allowing even small initial investments to grow substantially over the years.

Moreover, dividend stocks tend to exhibit less volatility compared to non-dividend-paying stocks. During market downturns, companies that pay dividends are often more resilient, as they provide a cushion of income for investors. This stability can be especially reassuring for parents and families who prioritize financial security. By including dividend stocks in an investment portfolio, individuals can mitigate risk while still participating in the potential growth of the stock market. This aspect is crucial for those who might be cautious about the fluctuations of other investment types, such as cryptocurrencies or small-cap stocks.

Another significant benefit of dividend stocks is their ability to provide a hedge against inflation. As the cost of living rises, dividend payouts can increase, helping investors maintain their purchasing power. This is particularly relevant for families facing rising expenses in areas such as education, healthcare, and housing. By choosing dividend stocks from established companies with a history of consistent payouts, investors can create a stream of income that not only supports current financial needs but also adapts to changing economic conditions.

Finally, dividend stocks align well with the principles of sustainable investing. Many companies that focus on dividends are also committed to long-term growth strategies and responsible business practices. For those interested in ethical investing, dividend stocks can serve as a means to support companies that prioritize sustainability while benefiting financially. As the market continues to evolve, the focus on sustainable and socially responsible investments is becoming increasingly important, making dividend stocks an attractive option for individuals who wish to invest with purpose while securing their financial future.

How to Select Dividend Growth Stocks

Selecting dividend growth stocks involves a systematic approach that combines research, analysis, and an understanding of the market landscape. Dividend growth stocks are shares of companies that not only pay dividends but also have a history of increasing those dividends over time. This makes them attractive to investors looking for both income and potential capital appreciation. For parents, teachers, and new moms and dads, understanding how to identify these stocks can be a valuable addition to their investment strategies.

The first step in selecting dividend growth stocks is to identify companies with a strong track record of dividend payments. Investors should look for firms that have consistently paid dividends for at least five to ten years, as this indicates stability and a commitment to returning capital to shareholders. Resources like financial news websites, stock screeners, and investment research platforms can provide valuable data on dividend history. It is also essential to evaluate the dividend yield, which is calculated by dividing the annual dividend payment by the stock price. A higher yield can be enticing, but it's important to analyze whether the yield is sustainable.

Next, investors should assess the company's financial health and growth prospects. Key financial metrics to consider include revenue growth, earnings per share (EPS), and cash flow. A company that generates strong cash flow is better positioned to maintain or increase its dividends. Additionally, examining the payout ratio, which is the percentage of earnings paid out as dividends, helps determine if a company is reinvesting enough in its business while also rewarding shareholders. A payout ratio under 60% is often considered sustainable, allowing room for future dividend increases.

Another critical factor is the company's competitive position within its industry. Understanding the market dynamics and the company's role can provide insights into its long-term viability. Companies with strong brand recognition, proprietary technology, or significant market share are often better equipped to navigate economic downturns and continue paying dividends. Furthermore, evaluating the management team's track record and their commitment to returning value to shareholders can also play a crucial role in selecting the right dividend growth stocks.

Finally, diversification is key to managing risk in a dividend growth investing strategy. Investors should aim to build a portfolio that includes stocks from various sectors and industries. This approach helps mitigate the impact of poor performance from any single stock or sector. Additionally, considering international dividend growth stocks can expose investors to opportunities beyond their domestic market, allowing for broader diversification and potential for higher returns. By following these steps, parents, teachers, and new investors can make informed decisions and create a resilient investment portfolio focused on long-term growth and income generation.

Global Dividend Growth Opportunities

Global dividend growth opportunities have become increasingly attractive for investors seeking stable income streams while participating in the potential for capital appreciation. As more investors look beyond their domestic markets, international dividend-paying stocks present a unique avenue for diversification and growth. These opportunities can be especially appealing to parents, teachers, and new families who are planning for long-term financial stability and are interested in sustainable investments that can benefit future generations.

One of the key advantages of investing in global dividend-paying stocks is the ability to tap into economies that exhibit strong growth potential. Emerging markets, in particular, often boast companies that are expanding rapidly and can provide robust dividend yields. These markets may not only offer higher returns but also the chance to invest in industries that align with sustainable and socially responsible practices, appealing to those who prioritize ethical investing alongside financial returns.

Moreover, global dividend growth opportunities can help mitigate risks associated with domestic economic fluctuations. By diversifying investments across different countries and sectors, investors can reduce their exposure to localized downturns. For families and educators looking to build a resilient investment portfolio, this strategy can serve as a buffer against economic uncertainties, ensuring a more stable income over time. It also allows for the exploration of small-cap stocks in various international markets, which can offer significant growth potential due to their agile business models.

Investors should also consider the impact of currency fluctuations on their dividend returns. While investing in foreign markets can introduce some volatility, it also provides the potential for enhanced returns when currency values shift favorably. This aspect is critical for individuals who are educating themselves about international investing and want to capitalize on the growth of global economies. Understanding how currency movements affect dividends can empower investors to make informed decisions that align with their long-term financial goals.

In conclusion, global dividend growth opportunities represent a compelling option for those looking to expand their investment horizons. By focusing on sustainable practices and diversifying across international markets, parents, teachers, and new parents can create a financial strategy that not only aims for growth but also fosters a responsible investment approach. As the global economy continues to evolve, staying informed about these opportunities will be key to achieving financial security for themselves and their families.

Chapter 6: Small-Cap Stock Investing

Understanding Small-Cap Stocks

Small-cap stocks represent companies with smaller market capitalizations, typically ranging from $300 million to $2 billion. These stocks are often characterized by their potential for rapid growth and higher volatility compared to larger, more established firms. Investors are drawn to small-cap stocks for their ability to deliver substantial returns, especially during economic recoveries or growth phases. Understanding the unique characteristics of these investments can empower parents, teachers, and new investors to make informed decisions that align with their financial goals.

One of the significant advantages of investing in small-cap stocks is the opportunity for substantial growth. Many small-cap companies are in the early stages of development, which means they have room to expand their market share and increase profitability. For college students and young families looking to build wealth over time, these stocks can provide an avenue for substantial returns. However, potential investors must also recognize that this growth comes with inherent risks, as smaller companies may be more sensitive to market fluctuations and economic downturns.

Additionally, small-cap stocks often operate in niche markets or innovative sectors, which can lead to exciting investment opportunities. These companies may focus on emerging technologies, sustainable practices, or unique services that cater to specific consumer needs. By investing in small-cap stocks, individuals can support businesses that align with their values, such as sustainable investing. This connection between personal beliefs and investment choices can be particularly appealing to parents and educators who wish to instill financial literacy and responsible investing practices in their children.

Investors should also be aware of the importance of thorough research when considering small-cap stocks. Unlike large-cap companies, which are frequently covered by financial analysts and the media, small-cap stocks may lack visibility and detailed information. Therefore, it is crucial for investors to conduct their own due diligence, analyzing financial statements, industry trends, and competitive advantages. This proactive approach not only enhances investment decisions but also fosters a deeper understanding of how various sectors operate within the international market.

Finally, it is important for aspiring investors to adopt a long-term perspective when navigating the world of small-cap stocks. While these investments can be more volatile in the short term, historical data shows that they often outperform their larger counterparts over extended periods. By maintaining a diversified portfolio that includes small-cap stocks, investors can potentially achieve greater overall returns while managing risk. This strategy can be particularly beneficial for new moms and dads planning for their children's futures, as it encourages a balanced approach to building wealth over time.

Advantages of Small-Cap Investing

Small-cap investing refers to purchasing stocks of companies with a market capitalization typically between $300 million and $2 billion. One of the primary advantages of investing in small-cap stocks is their potential for significant growth. Unlike large-cap companies that may have saturated their markets, small-cap companies often operate in niche sectors and have more room to expand. This growth potential is especially appealing for younger investors, such as college students or new parents, who may have a longer investment horizon and can afford to take on the risks associated with smaller firms.

Another advantage of small-cap investing is the opportunity for value discovery. Smaller companies are often overlooked by institutional investors and financial analysts, leading to a less efficient market. This inefficiency means that savvy investors can identify undervalued stocks before they gain mainstream attention. New moms and dads looking to build wealth for their children's future may find this aspect particularly enticing, as it allows them to invest in companies that may provide substantial returns as they grow and evolve.

Small-cap stocks can also offer diversification benefits to an investment portfolio. By adding small-cap equities, investors can balance their holdings, which may include larger, more established companies or other asset classes such as real estate or cryptocurrency. This diversification is crucial for managing risk, particularly for parents and teachers who may be looking to secure their financial futures while also educating the next generation about investment strategies. A well-rounded investment approach helps mitigate volatility and can lead to more stable returns over time.

Investing in small-cap companies can sometimes lead to higher returns than investing in larger, more established firms. Historical data has shown that small-cap stocks tend to outperform their large-cap counterparts over the long term. This trend can be appealing to those interested in dividend growth investing, as small-cap companies that experience rapid growth may eventually scale up their operations and start paying dividends to their shareholders. This can create a passive income stream that parents and educators can use for various financial goals, such as funding education or starting a business.

Finally, many small-cap companies are at the forefront of innovation and sustainability efforts. As the world increasingly focuses on sustainable practices, small-cap firms often lead the charge in developing new technologies and solutions. This aspect aligns well with the interests of parents and college students who are passionate about environmental and social issues. Investing in small-cap stocks that prioritize sustainability can contribute not only to personal financial goals but also to broader societal impacts, making it a compelling choice for those focused on ethical investing.

Identifying Promising Small-Cap Opportunities

Identifying promising small-cap opportunities requires a keen understanding of market dynamics and a careful analysis of potential investments. Small-cap stocks, typically defined as companies with a market capitalization between $300 million and $2 billion, often represent the engines of innovation and growth within the economy. For parents, teachers, college students, and new moms and dads looking to diversify their investment portfolios, small-cap stocks can provide significant upside potential, albeit with inherent risks. The key is to approach these investments with a well-informed strategy that takes into account both qualitative and quantitative factors.

One effective strategy for identifying promising small-cap stocks is to conduct thorough research on industry trends and emerging sectors. Sustainable investing has gained traction in recent years, with a growing number of small-cap companies focusing on environmentally friendly practices and products. Investors should explore businesses that not only demonstrate strong financial health but also align with the values of sustainability and social responsibility. By concentrating on companies that prioritize environmental, social, and governance (ESG) criteria, investors can uncover opportunities that are not only financially rewarding but also contribute positively to society.

Another avenue worth exploring is the potential of small-cap stocks in the realm of technology and innovation. Many small-cap companies are at the forefront of advancements in areas such as cryptocurrency, artificial intelligence, and renewable energy. These sectors are characterized by rapid growth and the potential for substantial returns. For example, new moms and dads might find intriguing opportunities in companies developing tech solutions that cater to parenting needs or education tools for children. By focusing on industries that are expected to thrive in the coming years, investors can position themselves to capitalize on emerging trends.

Assessing a small-cap company's financial health is crucial in the selection process. Investors should look for companies with strong balance sheets, consistent revenue growth, and robust cash flow. Financial metrics such as the price-to-earnings ratio, debt-to-equity ratio, and return on equity can provide insights into a company's performance and stability. Additionally, understanding dividend policies can be beneficial; companies that demonstrate a commitment to dividend growth can offer an extra layer of security and income potential. This is particularly appealing for parents and teachers who may be looking for investments that can provide fruitful returns over time.

Lastly, staying informed about the global market landscape is essential for identifying promising small-cap opportunities. International market investing opens up a world of possibilities, as small-cap companies in emerging markets can offer unique growth prospects that are not available in more developed economies. Investors should pay attention to geopolitical developments, currency fluctuations, and local economic conditions that can impact performance. By keeping a global perspective and being adaptable to changing market conditions, investors can uncover small-cap gems that may lead to substantial financial rewards while contributing to a more sustainable future.

Risks Associated with Small-Cap Investments

Investing in small-cap stocks can present enticing opportunities for growth, particularly for those looking to diversify their portfolios.

However, it is critical for investors, especially parents and educators guiding the next generation, to understand the associated risks before diving into this segment of the market. Small-cap companies, typically defined as those with a market capitalization between $300 million and $2 billion, often have limited resources and less established business models than their larger counterparts. This lack of stability can lead to significant fluctuations in stock prices, making small-cap investments inherently more volatile.

One of the primary risks associated with small-cap investments is their susceptibility to market fluctuations. These companies often operate within niche markets and may be heavily influenced by economic conditions or changes in consumer behavior. For instance, a small-cap firm reliant on a specific product can face dire consequences if that product falls out of favor or if a larger competitor enters the market. This volatility can be particularly concerning for new moms and dads who may be looking for a safer investment avenue to secure their family's financial future.

Another notable risk is the limited access to capital that small-cap companies often experience. Unlike larger firms, which can easily tap into various financing sources, small-cap companies may struggle to secure funding through traditional means, such as bank loans or public offerings. This financial constraint can hinder their growth potential and ability to weather economic downturns. Parents and teachers who are educating young investors must emphasize the importance of conducting thorough research on a company's financial health before making any investment decisions.

Liquidity is also a significant consideration when investing in small-cap stocks. These stocks are often less frequently traded, which can lead to wider bid-ask spreads and make it more challenging to buy or sell shares without impacting the stock's price. For college students or new investors who require flexibility in their investment strategies, this can be a critical factor. They must be prepared for the possibility that they may not be able to sell their shares quickly or at a desirable price, which can lead to unexpected losses.

Lastly, small-cap investments may lack the level of transparency and regulatory scrutiny that larger, established firms are subject to. Smaller companies might not have the same reporting standards or may not be required to disclose as much information to investors, leading to challenges in evaluating their true performance and potential. This information gap can be particularly daunting for parents and educators who wish to instill a sense of informed decision-making in young investors. Understanding these risks is essential for navigating the world of small-cap investments and making informed choices that align with their financial goals.

Chapter 7: International Market Investing

The Importance of Global Exposure

Global exposure is essential in today's interconnected world, where opportunities span beyond local borders. Understanding international markets provides individuals with diverse perspectives that enrich their knowledge and decision-making capabilities. For parents, teachers, college students, and new moms and dads, fostering a global mindset can significantly enhance their understanding of various investment avenues, including sustainable investing, cryptocurrency, real estate, and more. This awareness not only prepares them for a globalized economy but also equips them with the tools to make informed financial decisions.

One of the primary benefits of global exposure is the access to a wider range of investment opportunities. For instance, sustainable investing is gaining momentum worldwide, with numerous countries implementing eco-friendly initiatives. By exploring international markets, investors can identify companies leading in sustainability practices, thus aligning their financial goals with their values. Additionally, cryptocurrency has no geographical boundaries, and understanding its global implications can help investors navigate this rapidly evolving landscape, ensuring they do not miss out on potential gains.

Real estate investing is another area where global exposure proves invaluable. Different markets around the world offer unique opportunities for property investment, influenced by local economic conditions, cultural factors, and regulatory environments. For parents and new families, diversifying their investment portfolio by considering international real estate can provide stability and long-term growth. Moreover, understanding the dynamics of foreign markets can help mitigate risks associated with local economic downturns, making global exposure a crucial aspect of sound investment strategy.

Dividend growth investing benefits significantly from a global perspective as well. Companies with a consistent track record of increasing dividends are often found in diverse markets, and exposure to these international players can enhance an investor's income stream. For college students and young professionals, recognizing the potential of dividend growth investing in various countries can lead to better financial literacy and investment acumen. This knowledge fosters a proactive approach to personal finance, equipping them for future financial challenges.

Finally, small-cap stock investing is another realm where global exposure can yield significant rewards. Emerging markets often showcase small-cap companies with high growth potential. By understanding and participating in these markets, investors can capitalize on trends that may not yet be recognized in their local economies. Parents and teachers can encourage the next generation to explore these opportunities, emphasizing the importance of a global perspective in navigating investment landscapes. Ultimately, fostering global exposure prepares individuals to thrive in a world where the boundaries of opportunity are continually expanding.

Factors Influencing International Markets

International markets are influenced by a multitude of factors that can significantly affect investment opportunities and outcomes. Understanding these factors is crucial for individuals interested in sustainable investing, cryptocurrency, real estate, and other investment avenues. Economic conditions are paramount; fluctuations in a country's GDP, inflation rates, and employment levels can dictate market stability and growth potential. For instance, a robust economy may present favorable conditions for real estate investment, while a recession could lead to decreased property values and rental income.

Political stability and regulatory frameworks also play a vital role in shaping international markets. Countries with stable governments and transparent regulations tend to attract more foreign investment. Conversely, political instability or sudden regulatory changes can create uncertainty, making investors cautious. For example, a country that enacts favorable cryptocurrency regulations may draw tech-savvy investors, while another that imposes stringent restrictions may drive them away. It is essential for investors to remain informed about the political landscape and potential changes that could impact their investments.

Cultural factors and consumer behavior significantly influence market dynamics as well. Different regions have distinct values, preferences, and purchasing habits that can affect the success of products and services. For investors considering small-cap stocks or sustainable investments, understanding local market trends and cultural nuances can provide insights into which companies may thrive. Companies that align their offerings with local consumer expectations are likely to see better performance, making cultural awareness a critical component of international market investment strategies.

Global economic integration and trade relationships further impact international markets. Trade agreements, tariffs, and international relations can create opportunities or barriers for investors. For instance, a free trade agreement between countries can enhance the flow of goods and services, benefiting companies in those markets.

On the other hand, trade wars or sanctions may hinder growth prospects and increase risks associated with investing in those regions. Investors need to analyze how global economic policies affect the markets in which they are interested.

Finally, technological advancements are reshaping international markets at an unprecedented pace. Innovations in communication, finance, and logistics are making it easier for investors to access global markets and diversify their portfolios. Cryptocurrency, in particular, has emerged as a disruptive force, transforming traditional investment paradigms. Investors must stay abreast of technological trends and their potential implications for various sectors. As the world becomes more interconnected, understanding these factors will empower parents, teachers, students, and new moms and dads to make informed investment decisions in the ever-evolving international landscape.

Strategies for Investing Internationally

Investing internationally presents a wealth of opportunities for individuals and families looking to diversify their portfolios and harness the potential of global markets. One of the most effective strategies for investing internationally is to focus on sustainable investing. By prioritizing companies that prioritize environmental, social, and governance (ESG) criteria, investors can align their financial goals with their values. This strategy not only helps in building a better world but also taps into the growing demand for ethical investments. Research shows that companies with strong ESG practices often outperform their peers, making sustainable investing a compelling choice for parents and educators concerned about their legacy.

Cryptocurrency investing has emerged as another exciting avenue for international investment. With the rise of blockchain technology and digital currencies, investors can access global markets directly and often with lower barriers to entry. Parents and new moms and dads can educate themselves on the fundamentals of cryptocurrency and its potential for high returns while being mindful of the associated risks. Participating in international cryptocurrency markets allows investors to diversify their holdings beyond traditional assets, but it is essential to approach this space with caution and a solid understanding of market dynamics.

Real estate investing provides another strategic option for engaging in international markets. Investing in foreign real estate can offer significant rewards, including rental income and property appreciation. For families considering this path, it is important to research the local market conditions, regulations, and economic factors that may affect property values. Engaging with local real estate experts or agencies can provide valuable insights and help mitigate risks. Additionally, international real estate investment trusts (REITs) allow investors to gain exposure to global property markets without the complexities of direct ownership.

Dividend growth investing is a time-tested strategy that can also be applied to international markets. By focusing on companies that consistently increase their dividends over time, investors can build a reliable income stream and benefit from compounding returns. For parents and educators, this can serve as an excellent means of teaching financial responsibility to children. Exploring dividend-paying stocks in international markets allows investors to tap into different economic cycles and sectors, enhancing their overall portfolio resilience.

Finally, small-cap stock investing offers a unique opportunity to capitalize on the growth potential of emerging markets. Small-cap companies often have greater room for expansion compared to their larger counterparts, making them an attractive option for those looking to invest internationally. However, it is crucial to conduct thorough research and due diligence, given the potential volatility associated with smaller firms. By diversifying small-cap investments across various countries and sectors, families can harness the dynamic nature of international markets while balancing risk and reward effectively.

Tools and Resources for International Investors

Navigating the international investment landscape requires a robust set of tools and resources that can help investors make informed decisions. For parents, teachers, and college students looking to explore sustainable investing, cryptocurrency, real estate, and other niches, the right tools can streamline the process and enhance understanding. Financial news websites and investment platforms often provide valuable insights into global markets, offering real-time data, analysis, and educational resources. Websites like Bloomberg, Reuters, and Yahoo Finance serve as excellent starting points, providing access to up-to-date market news, expert opinions, and detailed reports on international investments.

For those interested in sustainable investing, specialized platforms are available that focus on environmental, social, and governance (ESG) criteria. Resources such as Sustainalytics and MSCI ESG Ratings allow investors to assess the sustainability performance of various companies. These tools provide insights into how companies align with responsible investment principles, which is essential for parents and educators who wish to teach children about the importance of ethical investing. Additionally, forums and online communities focused on sustainable investing can facilitate discussions and sharing of best practices among like-minded individuals.

Cryptocurrency investing has gained significant traction in recent years, and various resources cater to this niche. Cryptocurrency exchanges like Coinbase and Binance offer user-friendly platforms for buying, selling, and trading digital currencies. Furthermore, educational resources such as CoinMarketCap and CryptoCompare provide comprehensive guides and market analysis for new investors. For parents and new moms and dads who want to understand the fundamentals of cryptocurrencies, podcasts and online courses can serve as excellent tools to build foundational knowledge in this volatile yet promising market.

Real estate investing, particularly on an international scale, requires different sets of tools. Platforms like Zillow and Realtor.com can help investors identify properties, while international real estate firms can provide insights into local markets. Investing in real estate investment trusts (REITs) is another avenue, and resources such as Nareit offer valuable information on publicly traded REITs and their performance in global markets. Educational webinars and workshops can further empower parents and teachers to teach students about the dynamics of real estate markets, equipping them with practical knowledge that can be applied in future investment endeavors.

For those interested in dividend growth and small-cap stock investing, analytical tools like Morningstar and Seeking Alpha can provide in-depth research and stock analysis. These platforms offer filters to identify high-dividend stocks and small-cap opportunities across international markets. Moreover, financial literacy programs can help educate families about the importance of diversification and the potential risks associated with different investment strategies. By leveraging these tools and resources, individuals from various backgrounds can enhance their investment acumen and uncover global opportunities that align with their financial goals.

Chapter 8: Building a Global Investment Portfolio

Diversifying Across Niches

Diversifying across niches is a crucial strategy for anyone looking to secure their financial future and capitalize on the myriad opportunities present in the global market. By spreading investments across various sectors, individuals can mitigate risks while potentially enhancing their returns. This approach allows investors to not only safeguard their capital but also to benefit from the unique growth trajectories of different niches. For parents, teachers, and new moms and dads, understanding how to diversify effectively can provide a stable foundation for their families' financial health.

Sustainable investing has gained traction as more individuals seek to align their financial goals with their values. This niche focuses on companies that prioritize environmental, social, and governance (ESG) factors. By investing in sustainable businesses, investors not only contribute to societal well-being but also tap into a growing market trend. As consumers increasingly favor eco-friendly products and practices, sustainable investing presents an opportunity to benefit from companies that are likely to thrive in a future where sustainability is paramount.

Cryptocurrency investing represents another dynamic niche that appeals to many investors. With the rise of digital currencies, this market offers the potential for substantial returns, although it comes with higher volatility. For those willing to delve into the world of blockchain technology and digital assets, cryptocurrency can serve as a diversification tool that complements traditional investments. Educating oneself about different cryptocurrencies and their underlying technologies can empower investors to make informed decisions in this rapidly evolving landscape.

Real estate investing is a time-tested method of wealth accumulation that continues to attract interest across various demographics. Investing in properties provides not only potential rental income but also capital appreciation over time. This niche allows individuals, including college students and new parents, to leverage their investment by either acquiring properties directly or through real estate investment trusts (REITs). Real estate can serve as a hedge against inflation and offers a tangible asset that can be managed and improved, making it an appealing option for diverse investment portfolios.

Lastly, small-cap stock investing and international market investing offer unique opportunities for growth. Small-cap stocks, often overlooked, can provide significant upside potential as emerging companies grow and mature. Meanwhile, international market investing allows individuals to tap into global growth trends and diversify their exposure beyond domestic markets. By incorporating these niches into their investment strategies, parents, teachers, and students can create a more resilient portfolio that stands to benefit from a wide array of economic conditions. Understanding these diverse avenues not only enhances financial literacy but also prepares individuals for a more secure financial future.

Balancing Risk and Reward

Balancing risk and reward is a fundamental concept that resonates across various investment strategies. For parents, teachers, college students, and new moms and dads, understanding this balance is crucial as they navigate the complexities of investing, particularly in areas like sustainable investing, cryptocurrency, real estate, and more. Each investment avenue presents its own unique risk profile, and recognizing how to align these risks with potential rewards is essential for making informed financial decisions.

In sustainable investing, the focus is on generating positive social and environmental impacts alongside financial returns. While this strategy can yield substantial long-term rewards, it often involves navigating the inherent uncertainties associated with emerging industries and technologies. Parents and educators can play a vital role in guiding young investors to evaluate the sustainability of businesses, helping them assess not only the potential financial gains but also the broader implications of their investment choices. This approach fosters a mindset that prioritizes both profit and purpose, essential for a balanced investment strategy.

Cryptocurrency investing exemplifies the volatility that can accompany high-reward opportunities. The allure of significant returns attracts many, but the rapid fluctuations in cryptocurrency values can lead to substantial losses as well. For new moms and dads, understanding the technology and market dynamics behind cryptocurrencies is fundamental to making informed choices. Educating oneself about risk management strategies, such as diversifying within crypto assets or setting investment limits, can help mitigate potential downsides while still participating in this innovative space.

Real estate investing offers a more traditional path to wealth, often viewed as a safer bet compared to stocks or cryptocurrencies. However, it comes with its own set of risks, including market fluctuations, property management challenges, and the effects of economic downturns. For college students and young families looking to invest in real estate, it's crucial to conduct thorough research on market trends and property values. By weighing the potential for rental income and property appreciation against these risks, investors can create a more balanced portfolio that aligns with their financial goals and risk tolerance.

Dividend growth investing and small-cap stock investing represent two strategies that can provide a balance of steady income and growth potential. Dividend stocks offer regular income, which can be particularly appealing for new parents looking to build a financial safety net. Small-cap stocks, while riskier, can yield higher returns over time. By understanding the underlying fundamentals of these investments and the market conditions that affect them, investors can better navigate the balance between risk and reward. This knowledge empowers individuals to make strategic decisions that align with their financial aspirations and personal values in an increasingly complex global market.

Monitoring and Adjusting Your Portfolio

Monitoring and adjusting your investment portfolio is essential for ensuring that your financial goals remain aligned with market conditions and personal circumstances. As you navigate the complexities of sustainable investing, cryptocurrency, real estate, and other investment strategies, it's crucial to establish a routine for evaluating your portfolio's performance. This involves regularly reviewing your investments to assess their growth, risk levels, and how well they fit into your overall financial plan. By doing so, you can identify which assets are performing well, which may need to be trimmed, and where new opportunities might exist.

In the realm of sustainable investing, keeping track of environmental, social, and governance (ESG) criteria is vital. As the focus on sustainability grows, so does the importance of monitoring how your investments align with these values. Regularly assessing the companies in your portfolio for their adherence to ESG principles can help you make informed decisions about potential divestments or reinvestments. This proactive approach not only supports responsible investing but can also enhance long-term returns as companies that prioritize sustainability tend to perform better over time.

For those exploring the world of cryptocurrency, the landscape is particularly volatile and requires close attention. Prices can fluctuate dramatically within short periods, which necessitates a careful monitoring strategy. Setting alerts for significant market movements and staying informed about regulatory changes can provide valuable insights into when to buy or sell. Additionally, understanding the technological advancements and societal trends influencing cryptocurrency can better position you to make strategic adjustments that align with your investment goals and risk tolerance.

Real estate investing warrants its own set of monitoring practices. Keeping an eye on local market trends, interest rates, and economic indicators can significantly impact your real estate investments. Regular property evaluations and market comparisons will help determine if your assets are appreciating or depreciating in value. Furthermore, examining rental yields and occupancy rates will give you a clearer picture of your investment's performance. This ongoing assessment can inform decisions about whether to hold, sell, or invest in additional properties.

Lastly, monitoring small-cap stocks and international market investments involves a commitment to staying informed about various economic indicators, geopolitical events, and sector-specific developments. Small-cap stocks can offer significant growth potential, yet they may also come with increased volatility. Regularly reviewing your holdings, being aware of market sentiment, and adjusting your portfolio in response to changing conditions can help you mitigate risks while capitalizing on growth opportunities. By maintaining an adaptive mindset, you can ensure your investment strategy evolves alongside the dynamic international market landscape.

Long-Term Strategies for Success

In the pursuit of long-term financial success, it is crucial to adopt strategies that not only align with personal values but also anticipate the evolving landscape of global markets. For parents, teachers, and students, understanding sustainable investing can provide a pathway to build wealth while contributing positively to the environment and society. This approach emphasizes investing in companies that prioritize environmental, social, and governance (ESG) criteria, allowing investors to support businesses that align with their ethical standards. By engaging in sustainable investing, families can instill values of responsibility and foresight in younger generations, ensuring that their financial decisions reflect their commitment to a better world.

Cryptocurrency investing has emerged as a significant player in the global financial arena, offering unique opportunities for growth. While the volatility of cryptocurrencies can be daunting, a long-term strategy involves thorough research and a diversified portfolio. For new parents, educating their children about digital currencies can cultivate an understanding of emerging technologies and financial literacy. By incorporating cryptocurrency investments into their financial planning, families can position themselves at the forefront of this technological revolution, potentially reaping substantial rewards as the market matures.

Real estate investing remains a cornerstone of wealth-building strategies that can provide both passive income and capital appreciation. Families can benefit from understanding the dynamics of the international real estate market, especially in regions that are experiencing growth. By investing in rental properties or real estate investment trusts (REITs), individuals can create a steady stream of income that can be reinvested or saved for future needs. Moreover, teaching children about the importance of real estate investment fosters a sense of financial responsibility and awareness of the value of tangible assets.

Dividend growth investing is another strategy that can yield significant long-term benefits. This approach focuses on investing in companies with a strong track record of increasing their dividend payouts over time. For parents and educators, this strategy can serve as an excellent tool for teaching the principles of compounding and the importance of cash flow in personal finance. By highlighting companies that prioritize returning value to shareholders, families can illustrate the power of steady income generation, reinforcing the idea that building wealth is a gradual and disciplined process.

Finally, small-cap stock investing offers unique opportunities for those willing to take calculated risks. Small-cap companies, often overlooked by mainstream investors, can provide substantial growth potential as they expand in competitive markets. For college students and young professionals, investing in small-cap stocks can be a way to engage with the market while developing critical analytical skills. Emphasizing research and due diligence, this strategy encourages a proactive approach to investing and can lead to significant long-term financial rewards. By exploring these various investment avenues, families can cultivate a comprehensive understanding of the international market, equipping themselves and future generations for sustained financial success.

Chapter 9: Resources and Tools for Investors

Books and Publications on Investing

Books and publications on investing serve as essential resources for anyone looking to navigate the complex world of finance, especially for parents, educators, and new families keen on securing their financial futures. The literature available today encompasses a wide range of topics, from traditional investment strategies to innovative sectors like cryptocurrency and sustainable investing. These materials offer insights into various investment vehicles, helping readers understand their potential risks and rewards. By delving into these resources, individuals can equip themselves with the knowledge necessary to make informed decisions that align with their values and financial goals.

Sustainable investing has gained traction in recent years, prompting a surge in publications that discuss its principles and practices. Books that focus on environmental, social, and governance (ESG) criteria provide readers with frameworks for evaluating companies that prioritize sustainable practices. These texts often highlight case studies and data-driven analyses that underscore the financial viability of investing in green technologies and socially responsible firms. For parents and educators, understanding the impact of sustainable investing can be particularly significant, as it aligns with teaching future generations about the importance of ethical financial choices.

The emergence of cryptocurrency has also sparked a wealth of literature aimed at demystifying this digital asset class. Publications range from introductory guides that explain blockchain technology to advanced strategies for trading and investing in cryptocurrencies. These resources often emphasize the volatility and innovative potential of digital currencies, making them ideal for readers who are tech-savvy or adventurous with their investments. For new parents, knowledge in this area can be crucial, as it enables them to consider modern investment options that might yield substantial returns over time.

Real estate investing remains a time-tested strategy that many families find appealing. A plethora of books covers various aspects of real estate, from rental properties to flipping houses. These publications often include practical advice, market analysis, and tips for financing real estate ventures. For teachers, incorporating real estate concepts into financial literacy programs can help students grasp the importance of asset management and long-term wealth building. Additionally, parents can use these insights to instill a sense of financial responsibility and investment awareness in their children.

Lastly, the literature on small-cap stock investing and international market investing offers valuable insights for those looking to diversify their portfolios. Books focused on small-cap stocks often discuss the potential for significant growth and the associated risks, providing readers with strategies to identify promising companies. Conversely, publications on international markets encourage investors to think globally, exploring opportunities in emerging economies and foreign markets. By engaging with these texts, parents and educators can foster a broader understanding of investment strategies, empowering their families and students to explore a variety of financial avenues.

Online Courses and Webinars

Online courses and webinars have emerged as invaluable resources for individuals seeking to enhance their knowledge and skills in various investment niches, including sustainable investing, cryptocurrency investing, real estate investing, dividend growth investing, small-cap stock investing, and international market investing. These digital platforms offer flexibility and accessibility, allowing participants to learn at their own pace and from the comfort of their homes. As parents, teachers, and new moms and dads navigate their roles, these educational opportunities can empower them to make informed financial decisions and explore new avenues for generating wealth.

One of the key advantages of online courses is the breadth of topics covered. For instance, courses focused on sustainable investing teach individuals how to align their financial goals with their values, emphasizing the importance of environmental, social, and governance (ESG) factors. Similarly, cryptocurrency investing courses provide insights into the fundamentals of blockchain technology and the intricacies of investing in digital currencies. This knowledge is particularly relevant for new parents looking to secure their family's financial future or educators who wish to pass on valuable financial literacy to their students.

Webinars, often featuring industry experts, offer real-time interaction that can deepen understanding. Participants can ask questions and engage in discussions, making the learning experience more dynamic. These sessions frequently cover current trends and developments in the investment landscape. For example, a webinar on real estate investing might address emerging markets or innovative financing strategies, while a session on dividend growth investing could explore the best practices for selecting dividend-paying stocks. This immediate access to expert knowledge is crucial for those wanting to stay informed in a rapidly evolving market.

Furthermore, many online courses and webinars cater specifically to different experience levels, ensuring that both novices and seasoned investors find valuable content. Beginners can start with foundational courses that introduce basic concepts, while advanced investors can delve into specialized topics such as small-cap stock analysis or international market dynamics. This tiered approach to education makes it easier for individuals to progress at their own speed, building confidence as they expand their investment portfolios.

In addition to enhancing personal financial acumen, online courses and webinars foster a sense of community among participants. Networking opportunities arise as individuals connect with like-minded peers who share similar interests in investing. This collaborative environment encourages the sharing of ideas and experiences, enriching the overall learning process. As parents, teachers, and new moms and dads engage in these educational initiatives, they not only gain essential knowledge but also create networks that can support and inspire their investment journeys.

Investment Apps and Platforms

Investment apps and platforms have revolutionized the way individuals approach investing, making it more accessible and user-friendly for a diverse audience, including parents, teachers, and college students. These digital tools empower users to manage their investments with minimal barriers, allowing them to participate in various investment niches such as sustainable investing, cryptocurrency, and real estate. With the rise of mobile technology, potential investors can explore these opportunities at their fingertips, regardless of their prior knowledge or experience in the financial markets.

Sustainable investing has gained significant traction, driven by a growing awareness of environmental and social issues. Many investment platforms now offer features that allow users to filter and select investments based on environmental, social, and governance (ESG) criteria. Apps like Acorns and Betterment provide users with the option to invest in portfolios aligned with sustainable practices, making it easier for families to contribute to a healthier planet while potentially benefiting financially. As parents and educators emphasize the importance of sustainability, these platforms can also serve as educational tools for younger generations, fostering a sense of responsibility towards the environment.

Cryptocurrency investing has emerged as an exciting and volatile market, attracting a wide range of investors, including new moms and dads looking for alternative investment opportunities. Platforms like Coinbase and Binance offer user-friendly interfaces for buying, selling, and trading various cryptocurrencies. These apps often provide educational resources to help users understand the risks and benefits associated with digital currencies. For families, investing in cryptocurrency can be a way to diversify their portfolios, although it is crucial to approach this niche with caution and to stay informed about market trends and security measures.

Real estate investing, traditionally seen as a complex and capital-intensive endeavor, has become more accessible through investment platforms such as Fundrise and Roofstock. These apps allow users to invest in real estate projects or properties with lower minimum investments, making it feasible for families and individuals on a budget. By teaching the basics of real estate investment through these platforms, parents and educators can help cultivate financial literacy among students and young adults, preparing them to make informed investment decisions in the future.

Dividend growth investing is another avenue that appeals to families looking for stable, long-term investment opportunities. Apps like Robinhood and Webull offer easy access to stocks that pay dividends, allowing users to build a portfolio that generates passive income. This strategy can be particularly appealing for new parents aiming to secure their family's financial future. By understanding the principles of dividend investing and utilizing these platforms, families can create a sustainable income stream that might support their financial goals, such as funding education or retirement. Embracing the potential of these investment apps can empower individuals to take charge of their financial destinies in an increasingly complex global market.

Networking and Community Resources

Networking and community resources play a pivotal role in navigating the complex landscape of international markets, particularly for those interested in sustainable investing, cryptocurrency, real estate, and various investment strategies. For parents, teachers, and students alike, understanding how to leverage these resources can significantly enhance their investment knowledge and opportunities. Engaging with local and online communities allows individuals to share insights, learn from one another, and access valuable information that can inform their investment decisions.

One of the most effective ways to build a network is through participation in investment clubs and community education programs. These platforms often consist of individuals with differing levels of experience, creating an enriching environment for learning and discussion. Parents and educators can benefit immensely from these gatherings, cultivating a culture of financial literacy that can be passed down to future generations. Workshops and seminars focusing on sustainable investing and other niches encourage participants to explore innovative strategies while fostering relationships that can lead to collaborative investment opportunities.

Digital platforms also play a crucial role in networking for investors. Social media groups, online forums, and professional networks such as LinkedIn provide spaces where individuals can connect with industry experts and fellow investors. These virtual communities often facilitate discussions around emerging trends in cryptocurrency or the intricacies of dividend growth investing. By engaging with these platforms, new parents and college students can gain insights that might not be readily available through traditional educational channels, positioning themselves to make informed decisions in the international market.

Local co-working spaces and community centers frequently host events focused on investment education and networking. These initiatives can be particularly beneficial for new moms and dads seeking flexible learning opportunities that fit into their busy schedules. By attending meetups or educational sessions, they can connect with like-minded individuals who share their interests in small-cap stock investing or real estate strategies. Such connections can lead to mentorship opportunities or partnerships that enhance their understanding of the market while also providing moral support in the journey of investment.

Lastly, resource hubs like public libraries and community colleges often provide valuable materials and courses related to investing. These institutions can be a goldmine for parents and educators looking to deepen their understanding of sustainable and international market investing. By utilizing these resources, individuals can access expert-led workshops, relevant literature, and even one-on-one mentoring sessions. The synergy created through networking and community resource utilization not only enhances personal investment journeys but also contributes to a broader culture of financial empowerment within communities.

Chapter 10: Conclusion: Embracing Global Opportunities

The Future of Investing

The future of investing is being reshaped by several transformative trends that are making it essential for individuals to stay informed and adaptable. As parents, teachers, and new moms and dads seek to secure their financial futures, understanding these trends can help them make informed decisions. Sustainable investing, for instance, is gaining traction as more investors prioritize environmental, social, and governance (ESG) factors. This shift signifies a growing awareness of the impact investments can have on society and the planet, encouraging a new generation to align their financial goals with their values.

Cryptocurrency investing is another frontier that is capturing the attention of both seasoned investors and newcomers. Digital currencies like Bitcoin and Ethereum have opened up new avenues for wealth creation and diversification. As these assets become more mainstream, understanding their volatility and potential for growth is crucial. Parents and educators can play a pivotal role in educating young people about the risks and rewards associated with cryptocurrency, ensuring they are equipped to navigate this rapidly evolving landscape.

Real estate investing remains a time-tested method for building wealth, and its future looks promising. With the rise of technology, investing in real estate is becoming more accessible through platforms that allow fractional ownership and crowdfunding. This democratization of real estate investment opens doors for families and individuals who may have previously thought such opportunities were out of reach. Understanding market trends, property values, and the importance of location can empower investors to make sound decisions that benefit their long-term financial health.

Dividend growth investing is gaining momentum as investors search for reliable income streams amidst market volatility. This strategy focuses on companies that consistently increase their dividends, providing a passive income source that can be particularly beneficial for families planning for future expenses. By fostering an understanding of how to evaluate dividend stocks, individuals can build a portfolio that not only grows over time but also generates income to support their lifestyle and educational aspirations for their children.

Lastly, small-cap stock investing offers a unique opportunity for individuals looking to capitalize on the growth potential of emerging companies. While these stocks can be more volatile, they often present significant upside potential as they expand. Educating families on how to identify promising small-cap stocks and the importance of diversifying within this space can lead to substantial long-term gains. As the global market continues to evolve, embracing these diverse investment strategies can empower individuals to secure their financial futures while making informed, responsible choices that resonate with their values and aspirations.

Inspiring Stories of Successful Investors

In the realm of sustainable investing, one inspiring story is that of Sarah Johnson, a former teacher who transitioned from the classroom to becoming a successful investor focused on environmentally responsible companies. After attending a seminar on the impacts of climate change, Sarah recognized the potential for profit in the green economy. She began her journey by investing in renewable energy stocks and sustainable agriculture. Over time, her portfolio not only grew in value but also contributed positively to environmental initiatives. Sarah's story exemplifies how individuals can align their financial goals with their values, showing that sustainable investing is not just a trend but a viable path for long-term financial success.

Cryptocurrency investing has also produced remarkable success stories, one of which is that of David Kim, a new dad who started investing in Bitcoin during its early days. Initially skeptical, David took the plunge after conducting extensive research and attending online webinars. He invested a small portion of his savings, gradually increasing his stake as he learned more about blockchain technology and its potential. Over the years, his investment multiplied significantly, allowing him to secure a comfortable future for his family. David's journey highlights the importance of education and informed decision-making in navigating the often volatile world of cryptocurrencies.

Real estate investing has been a route to success for many, including the story of Maria Gonzalez, a college student who began her investment journey with a modest savings account. Maria discovered the potential of house hacking, where she purchased a duplex, lived in one unit, and rented out the other. This strategy not only covered her mortgage but also generated additional income, enabling her to reinvest in further properties. Today, Maria owns multiple rental properties and is well on her way to financial independence. Her experience demonstrates that with strategic planning and a willingness to learn, even those with limited resources can achieve significant success in real estate.

Dividend growth investing has transformed the financial futures of many, as illustrated by the story of John and Lisa, a couple who prioritized their children's education. They began investing in dividend-paying stocks after realizing the power of compounding returns. By reinvesting dividends over the years, they have built a robust portfolio that provides a steady income stream. Their approach has not only secured their children's educational needs but also instilled valuable lessons about financial responsibility and investing for the future. John and Lisa's success reflects the long-term benefits of disciplined investing and the importance of a well-thought-out strategy.

Small-cap stock investing is often overlooked, yet it offers substantial growth potential, as seen in the journey of Tim, a high school teacher. Tim dedicated time to researching emerging companies in technology and healthcare sectors. His initial investments in small-cap stocks yielded impressive returns, allowing him to diversify his portfolio significantly. By sharing his knowledge with students, Tim has created a ripple effect, inspiring them to explore the world of investing. His story serves as a reminder that with research and patience, investing in smaller companies can lead to extraordinary financial rewards, benefiting both individual investors and the broader economy.

Final Thoughts on Global Investment Strategies

Global investment strategies have evolved significantly in recent years, providing a wealth of opportunities for individuals and families seeking to secure their financial futures. As parents, teachers, and new moms and dads, understanding these strategies is crucial for making informed decisions that can benefit not only personal finances but also the broader community. This subchapter aims to distill the complexities of global investment into actionable insights, focusing on sustainable investing, cryptocurrency, real estate, dividend growth, small-cap stocks, and international markets.

Sustainable investing has gained traction as more investors recognize the importance of aligning their financial goals with their values. This approach not only seeks financial returns but also aims to generate positive social and environmental impact. For families and educators, engaging in sustainable investments can foster discussions about responsibility and stewardship, teaching younger generations about the importance of supporting companies that prioritize ethical practices and sustainability. This investment strategy empowers individuals to contribute to a more equitable and sustainable world while potentially reaping financial rewards.

Cryptocurrency investing represents another dynamic frontier in global markets. While the volatility associated with cryptocurrencies can be daunting, understanding the underlying technology and market principles can demystify this asset class. For parents and college students, exploring cryptocurrencies can serve as an educational opportunity about digital finance and innovation. This knowledge can be particularly valuable as the financial landscape continues to evolve, paving the way for future careers in technology and finance. However, it is essential to approach this investment with caution and thorough research, given its speculative nature.

Real estate investing remains a time-tested strategy for wealth accumulation, offering both stability and the potential for significant returns. Families interested in generating passive income or building equity should consider the benefits of diversifying their portfolios with real estate assets. Whether investing in rental properties, real estate investment trusts (REITs), or crowdfunding opportunities, understanding this market can open doors to financial security. Educators can play a pivotal role in teaching the principles of real estate investing, empowering students to think critically about property ownership and investment strategies.

Dividend growth investing and small-cap stock investing are two additional strategies that can offer appealing returns with different risk profiles. Dividend growth investing focuses on stable companies that consistently increase their dividend payouts, providing a reliable income stream that can be particularly beneficial for families planning for future expenses, such as education or retirement. On the other hand, small-cap stocks present opportunities for higher growth potential but with increased volatility. For new parents and young professionals, balancing these investments can be a great way to build a diversified portfolio that meets both short-term and long-term financial goals.

As we conclude this exploration of global investment strategies, it is clear that the opportunities available today are vast and varied. By understanding and engaging with sustainable investing, cryptocurrency, real estate, dividend growth, small-cap stocks, and international markets, individuals can create a robust financial future. The key lies in cultivating knowledge and awareness, empowering families and educators to make informed decisions that benefit both personal finances and the global community. Embracing these strategies can lay the foundation for a brighter and more secure future for upcoming generations.

www.ingramcontent.com/pod-product-compliance
Lightning Source LLC
Chambersburg PA
CBHW070415230526
45471CB00006B/2811